CUSTOM AND RACE TRUCKS

DAVID JACOBS

CUSTOM AND RACE TRUCKS

America's fastest and finest

Osprey Colour Series

Published in 1983 by Osprey Publishing Limited
12–14 Long Acre, London WC2E 9LP
Member company of the George Philip Group

British Library Cataloguing in Publication Data

Jacobs, David
    Custom and Race Trucks—(The Osprey colour series)
    1. Vans—customizing
    2. Title
    629.2'23   TL230

ISBN 0-85045-506-5

Editor Tim Parker

Design Grub Street

Printed in Hong Kong

The enthusiasm for American trucks lives on. Such has been the success of first AMERICAN TRUCKS and then AMERICAN TRUCKS 2, both by David Jacobs and both published within the Osprey Colour Series, that we have decided to maintain the American content but to jump sideways. CUSTOM AND RACE TRUCKS is the result.

CUSTOM AND RACE TRUCKS looks only at the very best of the customised, glitter trucks that may just be 'all show and no go'. At the same time we look at those fantastic cabovers and conventionals which are 'all go' — the track racers, or 'roundiround' flyers — yet are often 'all show' as well. We have two parts to this truck jamboree.

There's not a highway to be seen, just racing blacktop and showground festivities.

Enjoy the thunder of the world's largest race 'cars' and the shine of some of the finest customising ever seen. It's all colour and genuine Wild West fun, something that there's never enough of and never too much.

Not to spoil a good thing we have experience of in the past, we show yet another self portrait of photographer David Jacobs. This time also he has numerous people to thank, without any one of whom this project would never have come about. Thanks to Lizzy, Sue and Bugsy, Lois, Wendy (*Ham & High*). To all at *Overdrive* magazine at Englishtown. And *American Trucker* magazine especially Harm and Ryan. *Let's Go Truck Racing* and the North Carolina Motor Speedway for their incredible help and interest. And to the most courageous and exciting people you'll ever meet, the truck race drivers themselves.

Contents

Wreckers and utilities

Above Best wrecker in the world. Maybe that's going too far when you see the next ones

Left Unusual Autocar twin-steer wrecker. As effective at the drags as at dragging

Big wrecker with Hubbard Anchor — extending boom. Neat

Glorious Mack wrecker from Union City.
Grumpy bulldog will keep you busy

Custom refuse truck from Central Jersey
Carting. Where next can customising go?

Above Stars and stripes for a cement mixer?

Right Is this an Oshkosh front discharge mixer?

Following page Dusk at the drags as a refuse truck takes off . . .

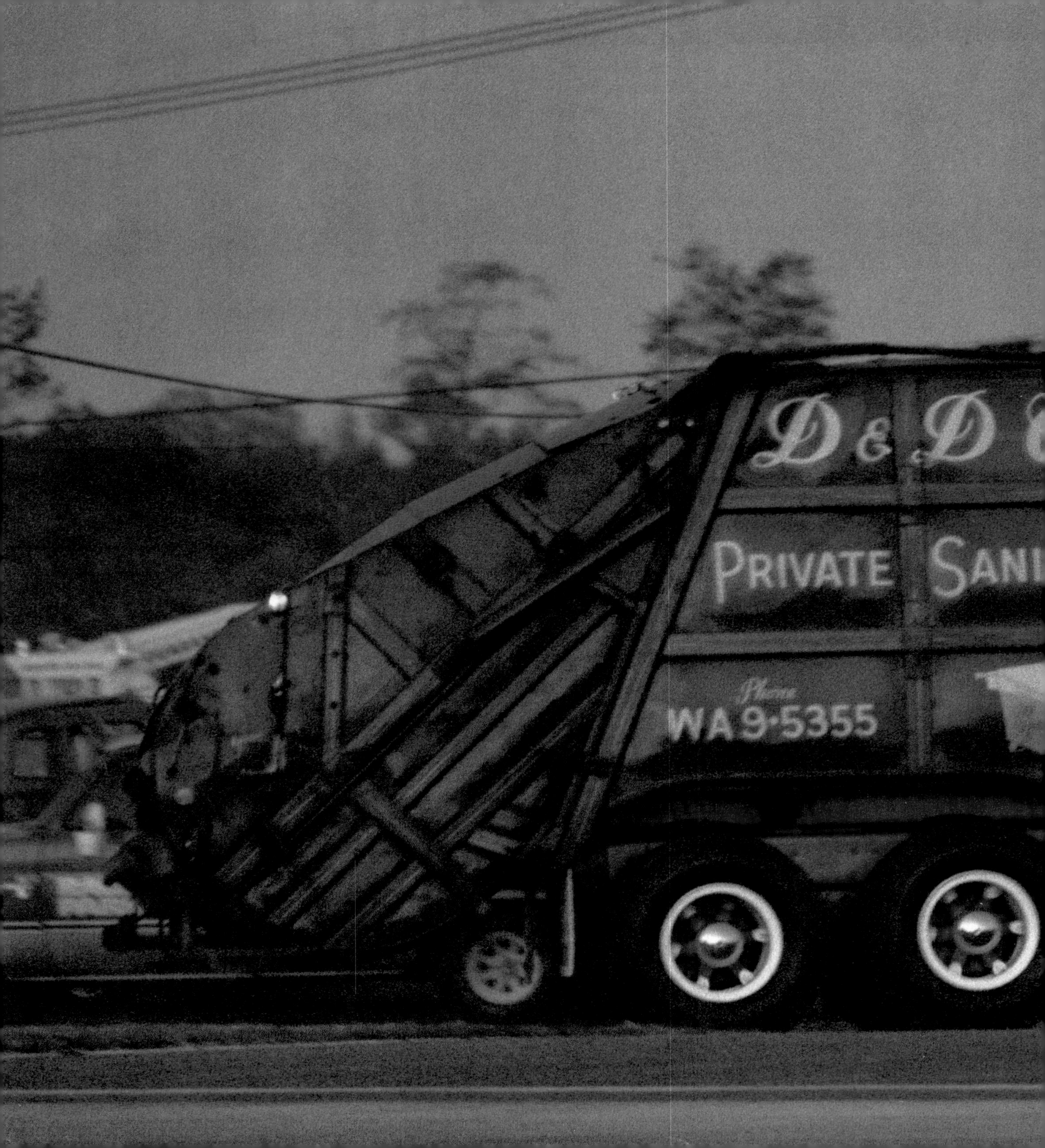
D & D
PRIVATE SANI
Phone
WA 9-5355

Above Mack mixer into the night

Right Glamour everywhere, apart from the Mack. *Penthouse* Pets to the right

Night racing. Swedish built refuse truck ready
for off

Oshkosh wrecker, winner and both *Penthouse* and *Playboy* promoters. Truck is spotless

Following page Big tipper from Autocar is typical of careful customising for workaday truck

International 5000 from Herbert Sand and
Gravel – East Coast racer with dent in that
chrome radiator shell

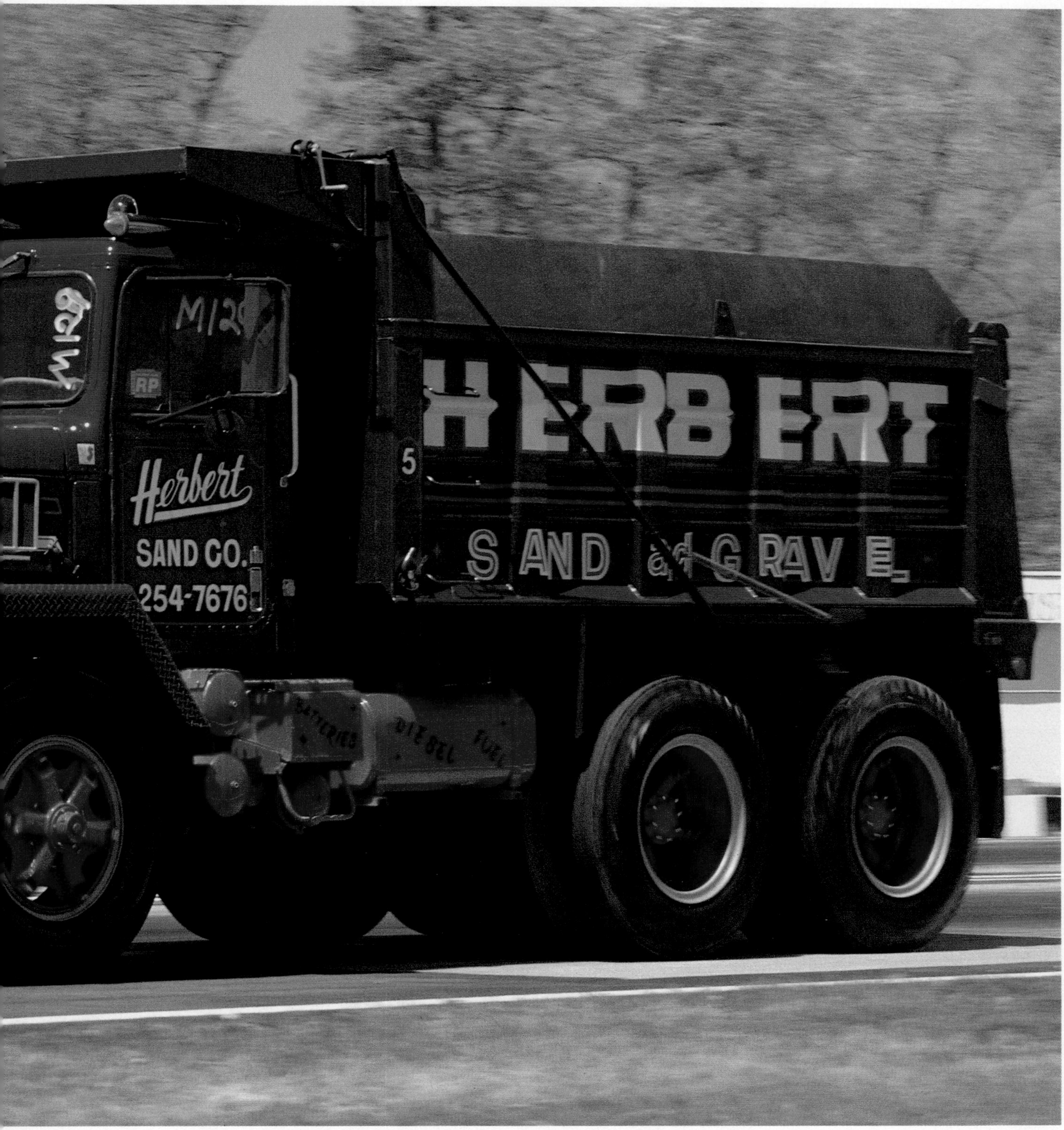
M129
Herbert
SAND CO.
254-7676
5
HERBERT

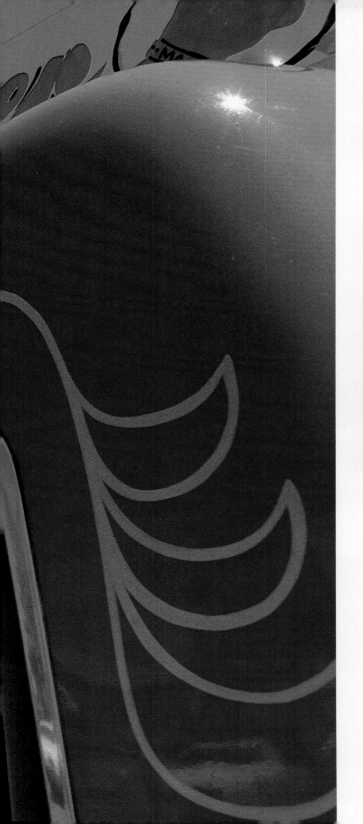

Cabs and fronts

Above Just neat

Left Pack of Mack

Left Lettering to make a typographer cry but a signwriter smile

Right Autocar with a big A

Below Rare International Harvester, registered as an historic

Following page *Slo Poke*. Lovely Oshkosh from Wisconsin. Superb paint belies go-anywhere reputation

Above British metalflake

Left Fantasy mural cab-back in a style more often seen on motorcycle tanks

Far left Anatomy out of perspective

33

Above Tasty GMC just on show. Paint quality is outstanding

Right Best in Show. It's a White

Above American style custom on a British owned Scania 142M. Still a rare scene in the UK

Right Mack drag

Above Night light

Left Rare Western Star from the White Truck
Group International. Crucifix lights

On track

Above All that's best in truck racing

Left Racing black top

Above Cement powder to kill the oil slicks left from practice

Right Line ahead and ready to run at the North Carolina Motor Speedway

Left Here's the crowd for the National Truck Racing Association's 250 mile meet. '82's event was called the Carolina 250 Bobtail

Above Just racing. Number 43 is Charles Reed who qualified 9th at 99.70 mph. Look at that antenna whip

Following page At speed. No. 97, Mike Adams, qualified second at over 105 mph. The two KWs in front were a little slower

Above Into the infield for Doyle Montgomery
of West Chester, Ohio

Left Into the banked turn. Sideways for one

Cabovers are unusual in track racing. Bill Oke
wasn't too fast

If you can't beat them, smoke them out . . .

. . . and then do it again

Forlorn Richard Davidson waits for the tow
truck to rescue his '72 GMC with 318 Detroit

UNION 76-ROCKINGHAM
PIT CREW RACE

//// NASCAR

Pit crew — refuel and screen clean for Randy
Johnson of North Carolina

Bob Lashley has run out of aluminium wheels
for this tyre change. Back to steel. Bob from
Louisiana was an over 100 mph front runner in
his '79 Kenworth with 230 Detroit

Following page Driver unhurt but the rig's
a mess

Off track

Above Number 2 for *The Flying Deu2ce*. Racer paint

Left Team spirit for number 2, Doyle Montgomery. His KW was fast

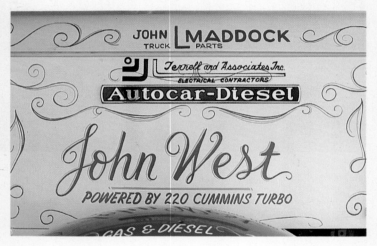

Top Fast motor

Above Georgia based John West didn't win

Right Colour co-ordination for Bob Lashley's Lincoln

Following page The big jump before the race . . .

. . . saw flames followed by Smokey flying
through the air and . . .

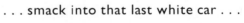

. . . smack into that last white car . . .

. . . as the wreckers approach to clear it all away. 'Hoss', or Hank Wise does this for a living!

65

Above 'Doc John', John Morrow of High Point, North Carolina sticks out his tongue

Right John West of Jonesboro, Georgia runs under his handle 'Abe'. His racer's smart

Left Running number 1 Richard Craig from Muncie, Indiana signs the programme for his fans. A front runner

Above Steve Slaybaugh with North American Van Lines sponsorship runs an '80 Kenworth with a 93 Cummins fitted. He qualified fifth

Following page Shade runner. A race truck pure and simple. In fact Charlie's winning rig

Left Race winner Charlie Baker from New Oxford, Pennsylvania ran away with the result. He's the world record holder — so the race programme says — at 132.86 mph

Above Talking over what might have happened

Following page In comes the Robert Bolus rig back to Chincilla, Penn. Nice outfit. It won't leave that way! Look back

Left The race day is over

Above Nightfall

Race truck technology

Above Twin turbo diesel power. On the mile circuit this one was a 100 mph performer

Left Immaculate diesel with custom paint on the block. It's an Autocar

79

This one's a working truck. Bud Albertson,
running at just 100 mph says 'You might see
me racing today and hauling freight tomorrow'

Above Turbo 1980 Kenworth with the pipework apart. Known as the 'Dixie Twister' Virgil Taylor's KW is a front runner

Left Can get hot in there

Top 'Hoodraiser' Bob Lashley beside *Little Toot* his '79 KW fitted with 230 Detroit, both haling from Pearl City, Mississipi

Above Come in number 10, your time is up

Right John West's Autocar racer again

Above The Richard Craig full time racer

Right Neat winner. Fast KW with racing tricks throughout being tech inspected

Above Corner weight?

Right You bend it, we'll mend it

Far right Fuel tech check. Regulations are tough

Following page Race tyre change. Quicker to hoist the front axle off the track

Left Hand cut slicks. Well almost. Truck racing tyres are a black art right now

Above Delicious alloy wheel rims save weight

Right Like NASCAR racers, these trucks require window nets for driver safety

Far right Nerf bars and safety clips for the windscreen

Below They go for seat belts and roll cages too

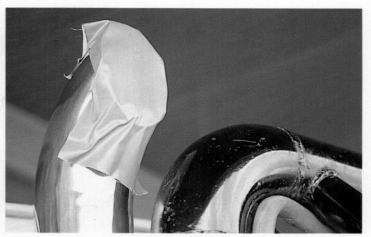

Top Don't want no foreign bodies down the pipes when not racing

Above Custom cover for glassless but netted window when no action

Left Serious stuff with cab roof spoilers

Above All racer; stark, smooth and built to win

Right I got pipes

Little drag'n custom

Above *Freightrain, Freightrain going so fast . . .*
(with apologies)

Left *Overdrive* Truckers Championship at
Raceway Park, Englishtown, NJ. A little drag
racing and a custom truck show. Here's a
wheel standing VW wagon

Above Class 0 – 6 wheel (two axle) fifth wheel tractor from 191 to 230 horsepower

Right *Mack the Knight* . . . (with more apologies)

Following page Lovely Ford conventional

Above *Big Mack . . .*

Right We have seen cabovers like this before. But it's still fun

Towing Specialists

Newburgh, N.Y.

Top Have a nice day . . .

Above Tidy

Left Funky art for a truck flap

Far left Historic, show International Harvester just playing

Following page Over 400 horsepower marked for this black chrome beauty

Left Wrecker controls

Right Rare Western Star with over 475 horsepower!

Following page *Miss Debbie*, 'Longhorn' Pete

Staggering Kenworth. Simple paint but just
the best

Lovely big Pete cabover too. Good for a
working rig

Above *Playboy*'s 'Playmate of the Month'
worked hard for the sponsors of the drag
meet and custom show. *Overdrive* magazine
believe in promotion. Look at those teeth

Right By contrast a British custom interior.
Jeremy Collet's Scammell

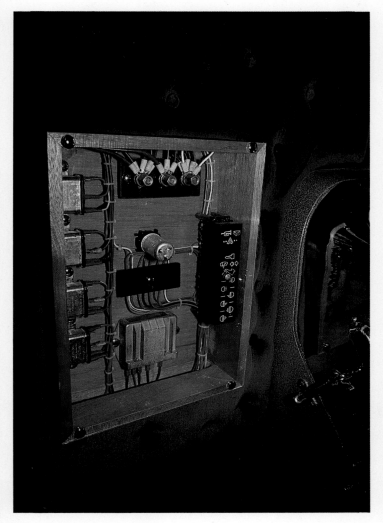

Above Nice electrics in conventional British truck style

Left More of the same. The equal of any around

Following page A taste of the British fairground. Not surprising with the origins of this rig coming from the showmen James Jennings and Sons of Devizes, England

American influence shows through

HW 541G

JEREMY COLLETT'S 'WILTSHIRE SHOWMAN'

Epilogue

Above Come in Mr Grimer. Dutch built Daf 2800 is a popular racer as well as freight hauler. Event took place at Northampton Stadium

Left English truck racing. Low key but exciting. Irish sourced Japanese Hino trounces Spanish sourced British Dodge. That's Harvey Smith pushing Malcolm Smith

British drag racing is low key too. Here an American GMC runs a Scammell cab over at Santa Pod

Following page Without wheels?